5/05 *22.00

973.7
Phi

DATE DUE

American Women
at War™

WOMEN CIVIL WAR SPIES OF THE CONFEDERACY

LARISSA PHILLIPS

The Rosen Publishing Group, Inc., New York

Published in 2004 by The Rosen Publishing Group, Inc.
29 East 21st Street, New York, NY 10010

Library of Congress Cataloging-in-Publication Data

Phillips, Larissa.
Women Civil War spies of the Confederacy/Larissa Phillips.—1st ed.
    p. cm.—(American women at war)
Summary: Details the lives of six women who fought to preserve the
Confederacy and the Southern way of life by serving as spies during
the Civil War. Includes bibliographical references and index.
ISBN 0-8239-4451-4 (lib. bdg.)
    1. Women spies—Confederate States of America—Biography—Juvenile
literature. 2. United States—History—Civil War, 1861-1865—Secret service—
Juvenile literature. 3. United States—History—Civil War, 1861-1865—
Participation, Female—Juvenile literature. 4. Confederate States of America—
Biography—Juvenile literature. 5. United States—History—Civil War,
1861-1865—Biography—Juvenile literature. [1. Spies. 2. Women—Biography.
3. United States—History—Civil War, 1861-1865—Secret service. 4. United
States—History—Civil War, 1861-1865—Participation, Female.]
    I. Title. II. Series.
E608.P47 2004
973.7'86'0922—dc22
                                                                    2003016715
Manufactured in the United States of America

On the front cover: clockwise from left: Belle Boyd, Rose O'Neal
Greenhow, Antonia Ford, and Mary Eugenia Surratt
On the back cover: a Confederate flag

Contents

INTRODUCTION

The Civil War (1861–1865) was the bloodiest war in the history of the United States. For a while, it looked as if the fledgling nation, an upstart country that had fought for its freedom, was doomed to fail. Even worse, its demise would come at the hands of its own citizens.

The U.S. government was divided between the federal government and the eleven Southern states that seceded from the Union. Some politicians and military leaders

defected to the Confederate States of America, the new government in the South. Families were shattered as brother fought against brother, father against son. Even generals who had been classmates as West Point were pitted against each other. Some battles produced tens of thousands of wounded soldiers. Many of them suffered agonizing deaths either on the field or at the hands of surgeons with dirty knives and operating tables made of wooden doors. Witnesses to the battlefields and hospital wards of the Civil War repeatedly described hellish scenes. (The Battle of Antietam, for example, which took place in Maryland on September 17, 1862, resulted in more than 23,000 deaths.) Even off the battlefield, violent draft riots and the sadistic treatment of prisoners of war seemed to mock the idealistic beginnings of the United States.

But while most people have heard about the soldiers and military leaders of the Confederacy, not many know about some of its female participants. Unlike the timeworn image of a Scarlett O'Hara–like war bride left at home to helplessly curse her fate, many Southern women of the 1860s were ready for action. Some of them, through the simple act of spying, made a significant impact on the war.

At some point, it seemed like everyone involved in the conflict, no matter his or her allegiance, was

This photograph, taken during the Civil War, shows Union troops standing guard on a Potomac River bridge that leads to Virginia. The Union wanted to prevent the infiltration of Confederate spies into Maryland. Western Maryland's coal industry allied itself with the North, but Virginia and southern Maryland, whose agricultural economy relied on slave labor, were loyal to the South.

spying on everyone else. The nature of the Civil War increased these activities. You could not tell by looking at or talking to people if they were on the Confederate or Union (Northern) side. Civilians from both sides gossiped with each other and with Union and Confederate soldiers.

At the start of the conflict, it was easy for the Southerners to believe that victory would be theirs. The South seemed to have many advantages over the North. A wealthy North Carolinian supposedly said, "A short time of conflict and the day is ours . . . They can never overcome us, never conquer us! We fight for our birthright! Freedom!"[1]

Geography played a key role in the South's assumption of an easy victory. The South's objective in the war was merely to stay put and defend its territory. The disadvantaged Union troops had to travel south, defeat the Southern troops, and occupy its territories.

The Southerners also had an advantage based on their lifestyle. The men who became Confederate soldiers were accustomed to a rural way of life. They had grown up riding horses, firing guns, and roughing it outdoors. Many of the Northerners were city dwellers who had to learn how to ride a horse and fire a gun, putting them at a disadvantage.

Almost immediately, the South happened to luck into an abundance of leadership talent. Robert E. Lee, Stonewall Jackson, and J. E. B. (Jeb) Stuart are among the greatest war leaders of all time. It took the North half the war to come up with powerful leaders of its own.

The South also had a particular advantage when it came to espionage. Even though Washington, D.C., remained part of the Union throughout the war, it was loaded with Southern loyalists who were already linked with powerful political circles. These loyalists were more than willing to betray an old friend for the sake of the South. Confederate spies began collecting information from old acquaintances and passing it on to Southern officers, often drastically affecting the outcome of key battles. Some of them, like Rose O'Neal Greenhow, intentionally remained in Washington to better conduct their spying activities.

When the Union army began occupying Southern towns and cities, more opportunities arose for espionage. The Union officers often stayed in local boardinghouses and even dined with local families. A teenage Belle Boyd gathered information by eavesdropping through a knothole in the floor of her aunt's boardinghouse. Others listened through doors. Some even cultivated so-called friendships with Union soldiers.

Among the greatest resources at the hands of female spies was their appearance. Even die-hard Yankee soldiers, committed to the cause of the Union, were not immune to a woman's beauty. Before the war, these young men and women might easily have flirted, danced, or even married. Just because the war was on, this mingling didn't necessarily stop. It just took on a more duplicitous nature.

Greenhow corresponded with at least one Union politician who foolishly shared classified information with her, often hidden within love letters. Virginia temptress Antonia Ford sometimes went riding with a Union general—before helping a Confederate guerrilla to capture him in the dead of night. Spunky Ginnie Moon, even after being arrested, accepted a dinner invitation from the very Union officer who had captured her. After the war, both Antonia Ford and Belle Boyd married men from the North.

Southern women contributed to the war in other ways, too. Social customs, which had kept women out of the nursing field (at the time, it was considered improper for a female nurse to tend to a male patient), were broken down out of necessity. Thousands of women flocked to the hospital wards to tend to the wounded, further crumbling these barriers.

Others went so far as to don uniforms and, posing as men, to enlist in the army. Still others accompanied their husbands on their march to war, becoming known as "daughters of the regiment."

One of the most well-known female Confederate soldiers was a woman named Loretta Velasquez. After her husband, Lieutenant Harry Buford, was killed in the war, Velasquez disguised herself and assumed his place in battle.

These women sometimes acted as mascots, nurses, flag-bearers, or even fellow warriors. (Some estimates claim that about 400 women disguised themselves as men to serve as soldiers in the Civil War, a few of them fighting alongside their husbands.)

But of all the women who found ways to work for the Confederate cause, the spies are perhaps the least acknowledged. Because of the nature of their work, many female spies were never discovered. Others who may have been revealed hardly received recognition. One historian notes that "Boyd, Greenhow, [and others] should be viewed as simply the most prominent among a vast multitude of women who showed their loyalty to their respective nations by carrying out secretive and dangerous deeds of espionage and resistance during the war."[2]

Whatever their exact numbers, it is clear that the social boundaries of the times could not discourage these women. In some ways they were prototypes of modern feminists. Too daring, too opinionated, and too active to be contained at home, they insisted on involvement. For many, the war was just the beginning; they went on to adventures as memoirists, actresses, journalists, and even, in one case, a Greenwich Village bohemian. But perhaps nothing could compare to their past exploits working for a cause for which they deeply believed—the Confederacy and the Southern way of life.

ROSE O'NEAL GREENHOW

Not much is known about the childhood of Rose O'Neal Greenhow. When she later wrote about her life, Greenhow preferred to focus on the details of the war and her fierce political opinions, rather than gauzy memories of a Southern childhood. What we know for sure is that this fiercely intelligent woman grew up to be a cunning spy for the Confederacy. She was considered by at least one contemporary to be "the most persuasive woman ever known in Washington," and "a woman of almost irresistible seductive powers."[1]

Born in Port Tobacco, Maryland, in 1817, Rose O'Neal was raised on her family's modest farm. As a teenager, she moved to her aunt's house in Washington, D.C., and immediately became entranced by the sophistication of urban life. A beautiful, intelligent young lady, she was welcomed into the city's most fashionable social circles.

Sometimes called "Wild Rose," she was soon sought after by many eligible young men. At the age of twenty-four, she married forty-three-year-old Dr. Robert Greenhow, an accomplished and wealthy Virginian. Together they had four daughters and enjoyed a prominent social life. They were friends with many rich and powerful people, including senators, politicians, and even presidents.

After her husband died an early death from an injury, Greenhow remained in Washington, a connected and powerful widow. She became known for her dinner parties, where she brought influential people together to dine in her beautiful brick home near the White House.

As the war approached, Greenhow had much to say. She was suspicious of the North's claim to care about slavery. She believed the North merely wanted to destroy the political and economic power of the South and that it was using the slavery issue as a vehicle to do so. She thought that Northerners wanted to drive the black population away and allow their own people to come in and fill the menial positions of the slave population. She also thought that President Abraham Lincoln had been unfairly elected.

When the Civil War began, Washington, D.C., was allied with the North. Greenhow was outraged. She vowed to do everything she could to protect the South that she so loved. Many people left Washington to join the Confederacy, but Greenhow remained behind to spy on the Union, using her social connections. In 1861, she joined forces with Lieutenant Colonel Thomas Jordan, the leader of an elaborate espionage ring. Through Jordan, Greenhow learned how to write messages in cipher and began gathering information from her many powerful acquaintances.

Greenhow became most famous for the influence she had on the First Battle of Bull Run

THE TRIANGLE TRADE

When it came to slavery, the New England Puritans came up with a grimly efficient trading system. Their ships left New England loaded with cotton and grain produced in the New World and headed straight for Africa to trade those goods for slaves. From Africa, the ships sailed to the sugar plantations in the West Indies. Here, if they could survive a few years of tropical disease and poor nutrition, the slaves were considered "broken in" and were taken, along with sugar, to the colonies for resale, completing the triangle.

Many Africans would die before they even reached the West Indies. "By any measure," says one historian, "it was an African holocaust."[2] As many as 4 to 5 million slaves were taken from Africa.

Northern abolitionists believed slavery was wrong, but they feared Southern power. When the cotton gin increased production of cotton in 1794, plantations needed more slaves. Then, in 1803, the Louisiana Purchase added to the number of slave states, giving more political power to the South. The Northerners also feared that the slave industry was reducing wages and taking jobs from white workers.

This engraving by F. O. C. Darby illustrates the first violent conflict between Union and Confederate soldiers at the First Battle of Bull Run (also called the First Battle of Manassas), which took place on July 21, 1861. The battle claimed nearly 5,000 casualties, some of whom were innocent civilian bystanders.

in July 1861. She learned that Union general Irvin McDowell was going to attack Southern troops near Manassas, Virginia. She also discovered how many troops he had and how those troops planned on traveling to Manassas. This was vital information. Greenhow sent a friend into Virginia with this information, dressed as a farm girl. The message, cleverly written in code, was rolled into the woman's hair, which was pinned up. The girl successfully delivered the message to Confederate general Pierre G. T. Beauregard. Just days later, the First Battle of Bull Run (also called the First Battle of Manassas) was fought. The Union suffered a stunning defeat, at least in part due to Greenhow's work.

Even though many people predicted a short war, the conflict continued to escalate. In Washington, all decorum and civility were falling to pieces. Greenhow wrote the following passage in her diary, "The streets were filled with armed and unarmed ruffians; women were afraid to go singly into the streets for fear of insult; curses and blasphemy rent the air, and no one would have been surprised at any hour at a general massacre of the peaceful inhabitants."[3]

Most women left the city, and Greenhow was urged to do so herself, but she refused: "At whatever peril, I resolved to remain, conscious of the great service I could render my country, my position giving me remarkable facilities for obtaining information."[4]

Despite living among enemies in the middle of a war, Greenhow refused to be intimidated. One day she was in the gallery of the U.S. Senate observing what she called the "solemn

THE FIRST BATTLE OF BULL RUN

As the Union pressed into Richmond, Virginia—the capital of the Confederacy—the first major battle of the war occurred in 1861. Confederate general Pierre G. T. Beauregard was blocking access to Richmond at the railroad junction in Manassas and along the little stream called Bull Run that ran through the town. Coming out of Alexandria, Virginia, Union troops marched toward Manassas, accompanied by citizens with picnic baskets and opera glasses, ready for a day of battle watching. Although it was assumed that the Union would easily win the battle with its large deployment, its soldiers were unprepared.

On July 21, the battle began. At first it seemed the Union's confidence was justified. But a Southern general named Joseph Johnston had brought backup troops to Manassas by train, evening out the odds. Among the newly arrived troops was one led by a Virginian general named Thomas Jackson. When the Confederate general Barred Bee told Jackson they were losing ground, Jackson reportedly replied that he would use bayonets if necessary to keep the Union troops back. According to legend, Bee then replied that Jackson and his

Virginians were standing behind him like a stone wall. (Jackson became known as Stonewall Jackson, and his troops were later called the Stonewall Brigade.)

Another legendary moment happened later: As fresh Confederate troops arrived, Jackson reportedly shouted at his men, asking them to charge the Union troops and yell ferociously. And so they did, and the phrase "rebel yell" was born. With it, a famous battle was ended. The Union troops—and the civilian spectators—retreated in a mad dash. A *New York World* journalist wrote: "But what a scene! . . . For three miles hosts of Federal troops were . . . fleeing along the road, but mostly through the lots on either side . . . Wounded men lying along the banks . . . appealed with raised hands to those who rode horses . . . but few regarded such petitions . . . Who ever saw such a flight?"[5]

In Washington, newspapers had already reported a Union victory. When the true outcome was realized, the city was thrown into a panic. Meanwhile, Southerners celebrated. More than a year later, on August 28 through 30, 1862, the Second Battle of Bull Run would be fought. Again, the Union army would be defeated.

farce of admitting as U.S. senators the bogus members from Western Virginia."[6] She made a comment regarding her opinion of the proceedings to a friend seated with her. Suddenly a Union officer in front of her turned around and threatened to report Greenhow for treason. She was indignant.

> I leaned forward and said deliberately, "My remarks were addressed to my companions, and not to you; and if I did not discover by your language that you must be ignorant of all the laws of good-breeding, I should take the number of your company and report you to your commanding officer to be punished for your impertinence!"[7]

For a long time, Greenhow continued her spying, often gathering valuable, detailed pieces of information. She knew that she was being followed and observed, but she merely became more cautious. Sometimes she could not resist having fun with the men who were trailing her. She and a friend would turn around suddenly; the person trailing them would turn also, and then Greenhow and her friend would follow him.

But one day she was stopped by two men as she entered her house. Allan Pinkerton, a

Chicago detective, had been hired by the Union and had formed the brand-new Secret Service. Increasingly worried about Greenhow's ability to land and convey military intelligence, on August 23, 1861, Pinkerton and his men placed her under arrest. With no warrant, they searched her house and took into custody every friend who came by to visit. Many of these people had just heard that she'd been arrested and had only stopped by to check on her. Greenhow was outraged. She wrote: "Men rushed with frantic haste into my chamber, into every sanctuary. My beds, drawers, and wardrobes were all upturned; soiled clothes were pounced upon with avidity, and mercilessly exposed; papers that had not seen the light for years were dragged forth."[8] Greenhow was strip-searched by a

A portrait of Rose Greenhow in 1855. A surviving letter to the *Washington Sentinel* from 1862 describes Greenhow's funeral as "a solemn and imposing spectacle," where soldiers, women, and children bowed their heads and cried.

woman detective and forced to watch as her house was torn apart. Ever cool under fire, she stayed calm and dignified the entire time.

Soon she was trying to figure out how to destroy the many sheets of paper still hidden undisturbed in her house that contained information. That night she sneaked into the library and took them down from the top shelf. She remembered that her strip search had not necessitated that she remove her stockings, so she had another woman who had been taken into custody conceal the notes in her own stockings. The next day, when the friend was released, the papers were taken to safety. Greenhow remained under house arrest for seven days, while every inch of her home was searched, including the furniture, which was taken apart.

After a week passed, it was announced that her house would be converted into a prison, with other prisoners joining her. With Greenhow in her suite of rooms were a friend named Miss Mackall, Greenhow's daughter Rose, and a servant. (Of Greenhow's three other daughters, one had recently died and two others lived in California.)

Although scrutinized and observed at every turn, Greenhow still managed to continue sending

CIVIL WAR PRISONS

At the start of the war, prisoners were treated fairly well—especially the women. Some women (if they were arrested at all) were put up in hotels, for fear that time spent in a real prison would be too damaging. Later, women were housed in actual prisons, but were often treated gently. Male officers who were imprisoned at the beginning of the war were also treated gallantly. As the war ground on, however, such civility disappeared. The infamous Libby Prison in Richmond held 1,200 Union soldiers in only eight rooms. Prisoners could be shot simply for going to a window to get light and air. But the worst was yet to come. In 1864, a 15-foot-tall (4.6 meters) wall was erected around 16 acres (6.5 hectares) of land in Georgia. Called Andersonville, it was designed to hold 10,000 men, but it eventually contained more than 33,000 Union prisoners in filthy, inhumane conditions. More than one-fourth of the prisoners who entered Andersonville died. After the war, Henry Wirz, the Confederate officer in charge of the camp, was convicted for his sadistic treatment of the prisoners and was later executed for his crimes.

A photograph of the Old Capitol Prison in Washington, D.C., on First and A Streets, taken during the Civil War. Rose Greenhow was once incarcerated here—along with fellow spy Belle Boyd. Built in 1800, the Old Capitol was first used as a tavern and a boarding house. When the Civil War began, the building, which was abandoned at the time, was turned into a prison. Today the United States Supreme Court Building rests at the site.

and receiving information. She survived on cheese and crackers, with no exercise, and very little sunlight. As the months passed, she grew weak and unhealthy.

On January 18, 1862, Greenhow and her eight-year-old daughter Rose were moved to the Old Capitol Prison in Washington, D.C. Here, conditions were terrible, and Greenhow was treated roughly and with great contempt by the guards. Meanwhile, her celebrity increased. Reporters came to the prison to interview her, and her house was described in detail in all the newspapers, both in the North and South. She later wrote about her prison experiences.

> The tedium of my prison life at this time was greater than I can depict, and I now also began to realise the fact that my physical health was being gradually undermined by want of exercise and want of proper food. A feeling of lassitude was stealing over me, and a nervous excitability which prevented me from sleeping. My child's health was failing alarmingly also. I had nothing to read, and even the newspapers were served or not, according to the caprice of my jailors, and were very sure to be withheld whenever they contained Southern news. My room swarmed with vermin, which the warm weather now caused to come out in myriads from their hiding-places; and, although at this time allowed the half-hour exercise in the prison yard, I could not regard it as relaxation.[9]

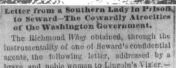

The *Richmond Whig* printed a letter from Rose Greenhow to William H. Seward, President Lincoln's secretary of state. Dated November 17, 1861, the letter describes the prison conditions she and other women were forced to endure.

In April 1862, Greenhow had a trial in which she nearly took control of the courtroom, accusing the court of treason. Some time after this, she was released and deported to Richmond, Virginia, where she was greeted by cheering crowds.

That summer, Confederate president Jefferson Davis sent Greenhow to Europe as a courier. She gathered diplomatic information for him, wrote her memoirs, and publicized the plight of the South. As in Washington, she enjoyed a brilliant social career in Europe, being received in the royal courts of both England and France. In 1864, she returned to the United States.

With important dispatches to deliver, Greenhow boarded the *Condor*, a British blockade-runner. In addition to her bag of mail, she had $3,000 worth of gold coins in a satchel, which was sewn into her clothing. It was not a smooth journey. At the mouth of Cape Fear River outside of Wilmington, North Carolina, a Union ship pursued the *Condor*. In its effort to escape, the *Condor* was forced aground on a sandbar on October 1. Determined not to be imprisoned again, Greenhow and two others boarded a lifeboat and tried to make it to the shore on their own. But they could not navigate the stormy seas. The lifeboat overturned. Greenhow might have been able to swim to shore

Photographer Matthew Brady captured this image of Rose Greenhow and her daughter in the Old Capitol Prison yard in 1862. Greenhow wrote in her autobiography about her daughter's plight and how "Little Rose" was forced from being an innocent child to one who was influenced by the harshness of prison life.

were it not for the gold sewn into her dress. There was no hope of surviving with such weight pulling her down. The famous spy met her death in the Atlantic Ocean before the war had even ended. Her body was found a few days later. In a coffin wrapped with a Confederate flag, she was later buried with military honors in the Oakdale Cemetery in Wilmington, North Carolina. Her epitaph, which is inscribed in marble below a cross that bears her name also reads that she was a bearer of messages to the Confederate government.

BELLE BOYD

As a debutante, Belle Boyd was not beautiful. Yet this Southern belle captured the hearts and minds of men on both sides of the battle lines. As a spy, she was not cunning or even particularly clever. Yet she executed daring missions, and through sheer bravado, helped the Confederacy win battles.

Maria Isabella Boyd was born in 1844, near Martinsburg, Virginia, in what is now West

Virginia. Her family was not particularly wealthy, but they were well connected, and Belle, as she was called, grew up adored and indulged by her parents. "I passed my childhood as all happy children usually do," she later wrote, "petted and caressed by a father and mother . . . and beloved by brothers and sister."[1]

The eldest of four children, Boyd was athletic, spirited, and naturally outspoken. When she was eleven years old, her parents denied her access to a dinner party they were hosting, saying she was not old enough. This was a decision they would soon regret. At the close of a genteel and well-appointed meal,

Belle Boyd was the most famous of the Confederate women spies. After her espionage career was over, Boyd's third husband, twenty-four-year-old Nathaniel Rue High, an actor, became Boyd's manager when she decided to return to the stage as an actress. She debuted in Toledo, Ohio, on February 22, 1886, with a dramatic monologue of her wartime exploits. Boyd's house on Pocahontas Street in Dallas, Texas, which she sold on July 29, 1887, was razed in 1963.

the guests were startled by a thunderous noise. The door to the dining room burst open, and Boyd charged in astride her horse. Amid the excitement, she asked sarcastically if her horse was old enough to join in the festivities. Already an excellent rider, she remained in perfect control of her animal.

Her parents may have been appalled, but the guests were delighted. One of them, a state official, was said to have remarked to Boyd's mother that a girl of such high spirits should not be punished but encouraged.

The following year, Boyd was sent to Mount Washington, a girls' finishing school outside of Baltimore. She excelled in her studies and remained outspoken and energetic. Since Maryland was on the border between the North and the South, students at the school held mixed, but impassioned views on the coming war. Naturally, Boyd was a vocal participant in the debates. She defended the South and the institution of slavery, which she believed was an imperfect but necessary part of society.

In 1859, Boyd turned fifteen. That same year, the attack at Harpers Ferry occurred, just fifteen miles (twenty-four kilometers) from her hometown of Martinsburg.

HARPERS FERRY

As slavery continued, many people worried about the possibility of a violent uprising by slaves. Instead, it was a white radical named John Brown who pushed tensions to the next level. Raised in Ohio, Brown was a devoutly religious minister who was opposed to slavery. Brown, along with some of his sons, formed a militia called the Liberty Guards and began fighting pro-slavery factions.

On the night of October 16, 1859, Brown and twenty-two men attacked the town of Harpers Ferry, Virginia. They occupied the town's federal arsenal and armory and took hostages. Brown's plan quickly deteriorated. The thousands of slaves he had expected to join the attack never came, and by the next day, a company of marines had arrived to demand his surrender. When Brown refused, the marines stormed the arsenal and captured him and his men. The trial began ten days later. Brown and his men were hanged on December 2, 1859.

The event became significant when abolitionist writers and politicians decided that Brown was a noble martyr. Meanwhile, the fears of the pro-slavery groups were intensified by initial rumors that thousands of slaves had been involved in the event.

At age sixteen, Boyd graduated from Mount
Washington. She spent the winter of 1860 to 1861
in Washington, D.C., chaperoned by her mother
and her slave, Eliza. A true social butterfly, Boyd
thrived as a debutante, going to parties, the the-
ater, and political events. She also acquired a
collection of suitors who were smitten with her
lively personality. That winter, she later wrote,
"for the last time for many years to come the
daughters of the North and the South commingled
in sisterly love and friendship."[2]

But the good times were about to end.
Abraham Lincoln had just been elected president,
and the tensions between the North and the South
increased. That same winter, seven states—
Alabama, Florida, Georgia, Louisiana, Mississippi,
South Carolina, and Texas—seceded from the
Union and set up a new nation: the Confederate
States of America. Virginia seceded from the
Union later, on April 17, 1861. Robert E. Lee, a
U.S. Army officer, resigned from the U.S. Army
and joined the army of Virginia. Mr. Boyd enlisted.

Boyd returned to Martinsburg and joined the
war effort with passion and dedication. She raised
money and acted as a nurse. But just because
there was a war going on, Boyd was not about to
sit at home. She shocked her friends by walking

At top, a photograph taken in 1860 of John Brown's Fort. Originally a firehouse, it became Brown's barricade location after he raided the local armory during the Harpers Ferry insurrection in 1859. Below, the same fort photographed in 2001. It is now a part of the Harpers Ferry National Historical Park in West Virginia.

the streets alone and frequently waved to both
Confederate and Union soldiers. Later she would
visit the military camps and even organize dances
with soldiers. But outrageous as this behavior was,
her notoriety had hardly begun.

Loyal to the Southern cause, Mrs. Boyd kept
a Confederate flag hung outside the Boyd house.
On July 4, 1861, a group of Union soldiers came
to the Boyd house to take it down. By the time
they arrived, Mrs. Boyd had hidden the flag.
Unsatisfied, the drunken soldiers began instead
trying to raise a Union flag in front of the Boyd
house. Boyd's normally reserved mother was
furious. "Men," she said to the rowdy group that
had taken over her house, "every member of my
household will die before that [Union] flag shall
be raised over us."[3] The soldiers cursed her. At
this, Boyd stepped forward with her arm raised,
a gun in hand. Before anyone knew what was
happening, she had shot and, by some accounts,
killed one of the Union soldiers. "I could stand it
no longer," she later wrote. "My indignation was
aroused beyond my control. My blood was literally boiling in my veins. I drew out my pistol
and shot him."[4]

Boyd was acquitted without being arrested,
but her house was put under watch. Totally

This print portrays Confederate commander Robert E. Lee surveying a battle scene in 1863. Lee's strategy included invading the North and occupying Cumberland Valley, Pennsylvania. He focused his troops on Gettysburg but was overwhelmingly defeated by Union general George Meade on July 3, 1863, in what became known as the Battle of Gettysburg, the largest battle of the Civil War.

THE MISSOURI COMPROMISE

Until 1818, the debate between Confederate states and Union states was a fair match, at eleven states on each side. But after the Louisiana Purchase the debate came to a head when the Missouri Territory petitioned for statehood. It was suggested that Missouri enter the Union as a free state, which would have thrown off the balance between the two sides. At the same time, Maine was also petitioning for statehood—as a free state. A politician named Henry Clay (a political model for Abraham Lincoln) suggested allowing Maine into the Union as a free state and Missouri as a slave state, with the condition that states later created from the Louisiana Purchase north of Missouri be free states. Since cotton could not grow north of Missouri, slaveholders accepted this compromise.

---

unfazed, she used the opportunity to flirt with and befriend the soldiers who were supposed to be monitoring her. Soon Boyd was pulling information from them. She sent Eliza to deliver the messages to the troops.

As a writer, Boyd was bold but not clever. She wrote the notes longhand, in her own writing. Since it didn't occur to her to use cipher (a symbolic code), one of her messages was soon intercepted by the Union army. Boyd was taken into Federal headquarters, but because of her age and gender, she was released with a mere warning. Unpunished, she left the Federal headquarters more committed than ever to serving the Confederate war effort.

Soon the war escalated. Boyd's parents sent her to stay with her aunt and uncle in Front Royal, Virginia. Little did they know that the real action was about to unfold in this town south of Martinsburg. Boyd used her aunt and uncle's hotel, which had been taken over by Union general Shields, as a base for her espionage exploits. One spring evening in 1862, a Union council was being held in the dining room. Boyd eavesdropped from above, lying in a closet with her ear pressed to a knothole that she had enlarged. When the meeting ended, she rode 14 miles (22.5 km) to tell Confederate general Ashby what had been said and was home before dawn.

Another evening, Boyd sat by the window reading to her grandmother and her cousin, not knowing that one of the greatest nights of her life was about to unfold. Suddenly, one of the servants entered in near hysterics, shouting that the rebels were coming to town.

Boyd dashed down to the street. There was chaos and confusion everywhere. Union soldiers were running in every direction. She stopped one of them and with the greatest sincerity begged to know what was happening. Unwittingly, he told her that the Confederate generals Jackson and Ewell were bringing their troops to town. He bragged to Boyd that the Union army had already captured some of the Confederate troops. The soldier explained the Union's battle plans and its intention to destroy the bridges and close the roads as the troops left town. Essentially, the Confederate soldiers were marching straight into a trap.

Boyd later wrote, "I was in possession of much important information, which, if I could only contrive to convey to General Jackson, I knew our victory would be secure. Without it I had every reason to anticipate defeat and disaster."[5]

Boyd quickly tied on a white bonnet and dashed outside. There were soldiers and civilians everywhere in the streets. She pushed through the throngs as fast as she could, dodging and darting, trying not to choke on the dust. She had ten miles (sixteen km) to run and many obstacles in her path. But she was hardly dressed for a day of bullet-dodging: "I had on a dark-blue dress, with a little fancy white apron over it; and this contrast of colors, being visible at a great distance, made me far more conspicuous than was just then agreeable."[6]

Artist Edwin Forbes created this drawing entitled *Front Royal, Virginia—the Union Army Under Banks Entering the Town*, in 1862. From Front Royal, Stonewall Jackson marched northwest toward Winchester hoping to cut off and destroy General Nathaniel Banks's troops. Jackson was partially successful. Banks, defeated at Winchester on May 25, 1862, still managed to escape.

As Boyd ran, some Union soldiers fired at her. The rifles blazed, some of the bullets hitting the ground around her, causing dust to get into her eyes. Other bullets singed her dress. She later wrote that it was miracle she survived. Still, she kept running. At one point, a shell burst upon the ground not twenty feet (six meters) from her. She had just enough time to throw herself onto the ground where she waited out the explosion.

"I shall never run again as I ran on that, to me, memorable day," she wrote. "Hope, fear, the love of life, and the determination to serve my country to the last, conspired to fill my heart with more than feminine courage, and to lend preter-natural strength and swiftness to my limbs."[7]

With her chest heaving, her muscles shaking, and her dress burnt and ragged from rifle fire, Boyd made it to the first of the Confederate troops. She saw an officer she recognized, Major Harry Douglas. As he held her hand, incredulous at the sight of this woman on the battlefield, she caught her breath and then delivered the message for which she had risked her life. Douglas galloped off to find General Jackson, and Boyd was free to go. Her mission was completed.

A portrait of Belle Boyd taken in 1862. Boyd often hid secret messages in her huge skirts because she knew that soldiers would never be so bold as to search them. The usual attire for women during the Civil War era consisted of voluminous skirts supported by hoops. The skirts sometimes measured thirty feet (nine meters) around. Even today, costume shops often call a costume with a big skirt a "Belle Boyd."

This painting of Stonewall Jackson was done by the artist Eliphalet F. Andrews. Because of his fame as a military strategist and leader, Jackson is a popular subject for Civil War historians. Today there is a Stonewall Jackson Museum and a shrine in Virginia.

The Confederates successfully defended the bridges, and Boyd's name became widely known. Just days later, Stonewall Jackson wrote to her: "I thank you, for myself and for the Army, for the immense service that you have rendered your country."[8]

After her stunning delivery at Front Royal, Boyd continued to act as a spy, carrying messages and letters to Richmond. But she was not as careful as she could have been. By now she was famous—the daring young rebel spy had been written about in newspapers throughout the North and South. On July 29, 1862, she was arrested by a U.S. Secret Service detective. He escorted her to Washington, D.C., and put her in the Old Capitol Prison.

Prison life was tolerable for Boyd. She was allowed to keep her own trunk of belongings and was told by the superintendent that so long as she remained in her own cell and did not communicate with the other prisoners, her door would remain unlocked. She was offered the use of a servant and given a choice of meals—often supplemented with sweets from admirers outside the prison walls. Still, there were decayed walls, bedding infested with lice and bedbugs, and a chill to the room.

On her first night in prison, the superintendent ushered in the detective chief, Lafayette C. Baker, who attempted to get a confession from Boyd. When he could not, he urged her to give an oath of allegiance to the Union. Boyd was offended. She firmly declared her refusal: "I would rather lie down in this prison and die, than leave it owing allegiance to such a government as yours. Now leave the room; for so thoroughly am I disgusted with your conduct towards me, that I cannot endure your presence longer."[9]

No sooner had she finished this tongue-lashing, than the other prisoners on her floor erupted in cheers and shouts. She hadn't realized that her door was open and her speech was audible

Secession Women in Custody.

"Fort Greenough," as they call it, where the secession women are shut up, is an ordinary brick house of three stories, on Sixteenth street, between K and L. As I strolled slowly by I could see very little indications of its prison character. A lazy sentinel was standing in front of it, to be sure, but he held his musket like an umbrella, and was busy chatting with some gossiping friend. There was a chair before the front door, but the door was closed, the lower windows looked uncommonly dirty, and there were no bars at all. The women are restricted to the second floor, and as I passed some of them were visible.

In the yard beside the house there is a tall round tent, and soldiers' blankets and accoutrements hang on the fences and the clothesline, while idle looking men in uniform loiter about the premises, as if they felt they had a right there. It must be rather tedious to have been shut up there as long as Mrs. Greenough has been—some three months, I believe. She has never, during all that time, been allowed to go out even for a short distance, and a request which she sent to the President some time ago to be allowed to go to church was refused. She is said to be an accomplished and fascinating woman, and one of the officers who was on duty out here is reported to have betrayed a degree of sympathy to

This news clipping from an unknown source was printed on November 29, 1861. The clipping describes "Fort Greenough"—the brick building in which Rose Greenhow was imprisoned for three months. According to the page, Greenhow had not been allowed outside of the prison gates nor was she allowed to attend church.

to all. Even the tough superintendent was taken with her charming fearlessness.

Boyd spent scarcely a month in prison before she was released and allowed to return to Virginia. Once home, she wasted no time resuming her espionage activities and capitalizing on her fame. The day after she arrived home, she rode out to the encampment where General Jackson could be found. Here she received a welcome that made all the danger she'd faced seem worthwhile. "As I dismounted at the door of his tent," she later wrote, "he came out, and, gently placing his hands upon my head, assured me of the pleasure he felt at seeing me once more well and free. Our interview was of necessity short, for the demands upon his valuable time were incessant; but his fervent 'God bless you, my child,' will never be obliterated from my memory, as long as Providence shall be pleased to allow it to retain its power."[10]

Around this time, there was word of President Lincoln's Emancipation Proclamation, which called for the end of slavery in the United States. This declaration added fuel to the intensity of the war. On General Jackson's advice, Boyd moved to Winchester and there received a commission as captain and honorary aide-de-camp to Jackson. She wrote, "[T]henceforth I enjoyed the respect paid to an officer by soldiers."[11] After some months of enjoying this, the Union soldiers approached, and Boyd restlessly moved about the South before returning home.

But Martinsburg was soon placed under Federal occupation, and Boyd was arrested. Later, she was summoned to Washington and put into Carroll Prison. As an inmate, she made friends with the other women, flirted with the guards, and sang Southern songs in an impassioned voice for all to hear. One night she was surprised when an arrow flew through the window and landed on the opposite wall. A letter was attached, expressing sympathy and friendship. It gave Boyd instructions for how to correspond secretly with "C.H.," the writer of the letter. In this manner, she was able to communicate with the outside world and exasperate the guards. They knew she was in communication with someone, but they could never catch her in the act.

Eventually, prison life wore Boyd down, and she contracted typhoid fever. After many weeks, she recovered—just in time to be sentenced to hard labor at the Fitchburg, Massachusetts, jail for the rest of the war. Under her father's influence, her

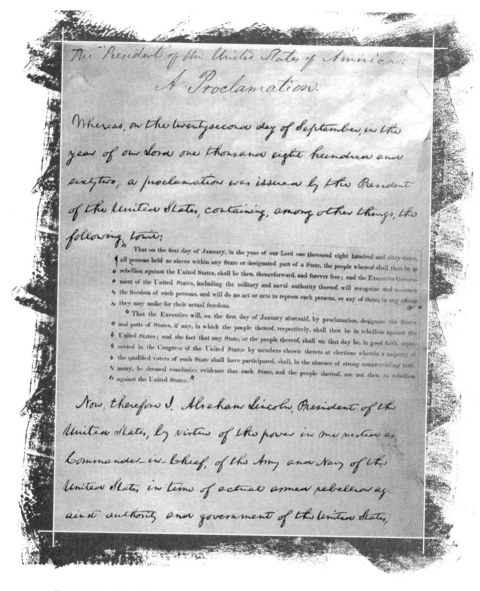

This is President Lincoln's final draft of the Emancipation Proclamation, dated January 1, 1863. The printed sections are from the first draft from September 1862. Parts of the superscription are written by a clerk. The rest is in the hand of President Lincoln.

sentence was reduced to banishment from the North for the duration of the war. This was more of a hardship than it might seem. Since Virginia had split into Virginia and West Virginia, Boyd's hometown of Martinsburg was now in the North.

On December 1, 1863, she was released from Carroll Prison and sent to Richmond. No sooner had she arrived in the city than she learned her father had died. Although she appealed to many powerful figures, Boyd was unable to receive permission to visit Martinsburg to pay her last respects to her father.

Distraught and discouraged, Boyd had the idea of going to Europe, where she could act as a courier for the Confederate cause. On the way, she met a Federal officer, Sam Hardinge. Their shipboard romance soon escalated, and the two were married in England. However, Hardinge returned to the United States almost immediately and died on his way back to London, perhaps on a sunken ship. The details of his death are unclear.

Alone in England and expecting a child, Boyd decided to write about her experiences to support herself. In May 1865, *Belle Boyd, in Camp and Prison* was published in London. It was well received and soon published in the United States.

The following year, she turned to the stage, playing the lead female role in a small play. That was also the year her daughter Grace was born and the year that President Andrew Johnson issued a Proclamation of Amnesty, which allowed her to return home.

She continued her theatrical career until the age of twenty-five. At that time, she married a successful businessman named John Swainston Hammond. The newlyweds moved to California and had three more children. Boyd divorced Hammond in 1884, and at forty-one years of age, she remarried yet again. As her new husband was an actor, his income was insufficient to support Boyd, and she returned to the stage.

BELLE BOYD,

IN

CAMP AND PRISON.

With an Introduction

BY A FRIEND OF THE SOUTH.

IN TWO VOLUMES.

VOL. I.

LONDON:
SAUNDERS, OTLEY, AND CO.,
66 BROOK STREET, W.
1865.

In order to make some money, Belle Boyd decided to write a memoir of her life as a spy. To the left is the title page of Boyd's autobiography, *Belle Boyd, in Camp and Prison*, Volume 1. The book can be found in its electronic version at the University of North Carolina at Chapel Hill Libraries.

This time she recited monologues about her exploits as a spy.

In June 1900, Belle Boyd suffered a heart attack and died. She was fifty-six years old. To say that she had lived life to the fullest and pushed the limits of what society expected of a woman would hardly be an exaggeration.

ANTONIA FORD

When the war started, Antonia Ford was in the comfort of a wealthy home near Fairfax, Virginia. Born in 1838, she had grown up in an environment with more privilege than many other well-known women spies. She was the beautiful daughter of a successful merchant. But this young lady of leisure was not content to spend the war sitting on a velvet couch and entertaining admirers.

Known for her beauty and her good manners,

A portrait of Antonia Ford (1838–1871) as taken by O. H. Willard. Ford was incarcerated in the Old Capitol Prison as a Confederate spy. She was thought to have aided in the capture of E. W. Stoughton by Mosby's Rangers in 1863. Ford ended up marrying her captor, Union army major Joseph C. Willard, less than one year after her imprisonment.

Ford embodied the personality of a cunning Southern spy, with charm that could make a soldier spill secrets. One historian says that Ford "spent no small part of her time in primping before a large looking-glass in her room trying on one dress after another, arranging her beautiful dark blond hair and posing with her gorgeously colored fan. She is said to have cultivated a voice so sweet and subdued as to add to her seductive appeal."[1]

But Ford was also a fervent supporter of the Confederacy. Her brother was a member of the artillery company of General "Jeb" Stuart, and she soon found herself sitting down to dinner

with Stuart and his scout, a dangerous Confederate private named John Singleton Mosby. Because Stuart's cavalry was posted near the Ford home in Fairfax, Stuart

A nineteenth-century photo of John Singleton Mosby (1833–1916). Mosby was an American colonel in the Civil War. In 1878, he served as an attorney and a United States consul to Hong Kong.

In 1863, George S. Cook took this famous photograph of Confederate general James "Jeb" Stuart (1833–1864). Stuart fought at the Battle of Bull Run in 1861 and the Battle of Fredericksburg in 1862. Stuart was an experienced fighter, having also fought against Native Americans. And as first lieutenant in the 1st Cavalry, he carried orders for Robert E. Lee to proceed to Harpers Ferry and crush John Brown's raid.

and Mosby were frequent guests there during the early part of the war. Stuart was soon fond of this young woman. Not only was she a delightful dining companion, but she was also a passionate supporter.

In October 1861, Stuart presented Ford with a document that named her as an honorary member of his staff. One witness later said that while the document was official in nature, the presentation was playful and somewhat in jest.[2] Just twenty-eight years of age when the war began, Stuart was known for his brilliant leadership as well as for his flamboyant style. It is easy to imagine him presenting a woman with a mock certificate.

Regardless of the intention, this commission would eventually have far-reaching effects on Ford's career as a spy.

In June 1861, the Army of the Potomac left Washington, D.C., and headed for what would become the First Battle of Bull Run. On its way, the army went through Fairfax Courthouse. A fevered skirmish led to the death of John Quincy Marr, the

A group of Union cavalrymen gather around the Fairfax Courthouse in Virginia during the summer of 1863. At this point in the war, Lee's army was moving north, pursued by Union forces.

THE SECOND BATTLE OF BULL RUN, FOUGHT AUG? 29TH 1862.

This Currier and Ives print from 1862 is housed at the Library of Congress Prints and Photographs Division in Washington, D.C. It is a colorful depiction of the Second Battle of Bull Run, fought on August 28 and 29, 1862. It portrays the Union forces, with their flag waving high, overtaking Confederate forces.

first Confederate officer to die in battle. After the brief fight, Ford watched as her beloved Southern troops left Fairfax and Union troops took over. The Union soldiers moved in to the Ford home and used it as a boardinghouse, just as their Confederate counterparts had done. It was there that Ford began her career as a spy. Using her charm on the Union soldiers staying in her family's home, she carefully pulled information from them and gave those facts to Stuart.

One day the Yankee officers ordered a search of the local houses. Ford caught wind of the inspection in time to make some preparations. When the soldiers arrived, they found her sitting in her parlor, looking harmless, with her skirts arranged artfully about her. She read and fanned herself as the soldiers searched the room. When they were almost finished, an officer asked her to stand. Ford acted as offended as if he had slapped her. "I thought not even a Yankee would expect a Southern woman to rise for him,"[3] she said. The soldier backed down sheepishly, leaving Ford's documents safely hidden under her skirts.

Right before the Second Battle of Bull Run in August 1862, Ford saved Southern troops from certain defeat by eavesdropping on Union officers. She learned beforehand that they planned to use Confederate colors to draw the Confederate soldiers away from their assigned positions. When she could find no one to deliver the message about the Union's plan for her, she set out to deliver it herself. Ford climbed into a carriage alone and drove twenty miles (thirty-two km) through the rain and directly past Union troops to deliver the information to Stuart.

But her greatest coup was yet to come. When the Union general Edwin Stoughton set up headquarters at Fairfax Courthouse and began

This engraving, *General Stuart's New Aide*, features a female on horseback and was printed in *Harper's Weekly* on April 4, 1863. While illustrations like this tended to poke fun at women who did military work, their contributions were invaluable for both sides during the Civil War.

gathering troops there, Ford informed Stuart and Mosby of the Union troops' movements. Stuart and Mosby were busy bombarding Stoughton's men with sudden attacks and sneak raids followed by stealthy withdrawals. It is likely that Ford helped them to avoid being captured, as Stuart and Mosby informed their troops not be lured away from their original positions.

At the same time, Ford was on friendly terms with Union general Stoughton, going for rides in the country with him and causing much speculation and gossip among his men. Once, she and Stoughton met Mosby in the forest. Since Stoughton did not know it was Mosby, Ford calmly introduced him as a local friend of hers. On another occasion, it was said that she had entertained Mosby in her home.

On March 8, 1863, Stoughton, who was just twenty-four years old and had a reputation as a womanizer and a drinker, hosted a party at a local home in Fairfax. Because of the party, Union security was lax, and because there was rain that night, outdoor noises were muffled. It was a perfect night for a Mosby-style raid. After assembling in the forest, Mosby and his men descended upon the town. Telegraph wires were cut. Prized horses were stolen. Union officers were taken prisoner. Later that night, Mosby himself stole into Stoughton's bedroom. The general was asleep, with empty champagne bottles strewn about his room. According to some accounts, Mosby lifted the general's nightshirt and smacked him on the rear. "Did you ever hear of Mosby?" he asked the sputtering young general. Stoughton sat up in bed and exclaimed, "Yes! You've caught him?" Mosby grinned in the dark. "He's caught you!"[4] Stoughton's capture led to his arrest and imprisonment and was a humiliating blow to the Union troops.

Union officers were incensed. Under great pressure to lay blame, the U.S. Secret Service chief, Lafayette Baker, immediately suspected espionage. He wrote the following in a report about the incident.

> The time, circumstances, and mode of this attack and surprise, the positive and accurate knowledge in possession of the rebel leader, of the numbers and position of our forces, of the exact localities of officers' quarters, and depots of Government property, all pointed unmistakably to the existence of traitors and spies with our lines.[5]

Although Mosby insisted that Ford had not supplied him with information, she remained a primary suspect. Because of this and other suspicions, Baker and his men devised a plan to catch her. A female Union spy, Frankie Abel, posed as a refugee from New Orleans. Abel showed up in Fairfax in ragged clothes and deceived most of the townspeople, but no one more so than Ford and her family. The Fords took Abel in, dressed her in fine clothing, and made her comfortable in their home. She formed a friendship with Ford, and they traded stories about their exploits in service to the Confederacy. At one point, Ford showed off her commission from General Stuart.

This was the hard evidence linking Ford to treasonable activity. On May 3, 1863, a few days after Abel left, Ford and her father were placed under arrest. Ford's father was released quickly, but Ford remained in prison until May 20, when she was released in a prisoner exchange. It was only shortly after that, though, that she was arrested again and taken to the Old Capitol Prison in Washington, D.C.

While in prison, she enjoyed one great advantage over the other prisoners: the swooning attention of a handsome Union officer, Major Joseph C. Willard. Back in Fairfax, where Willard had been the provost marshal, he had been an admirer of Ford's. When she was placed under arrest, by chance he was assigned to escort her to prison. He then began campaigning for her release. Willard was successful, and Ford was released in September 1863. Seven months later, on March 10, 1864, they married.

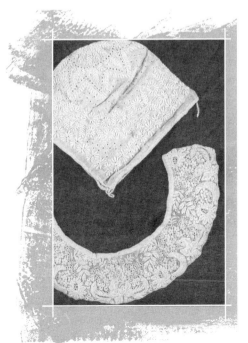

This lace cap and collar were made by Antonia Ford while she was in prison charged with spying for the Confederacy in 1863. Caps such as this were usually worn by older women during this time.

Ford later wrote to Willard of their first meeting, "I think fate has a good deal to do with us . . . It seems I was literally thrown in your way by a power above us—call it Destiny."[6] They had three children, two of whom died in infancy. After seven years, Ford died and was buried in Oak Hill Cemetery in Washington, D.C. Some believed that her early death was caused by her harsh confinement in the Old Capitol Prison, after which she had never regained her health; others say it was a consequence of childbearing. Her husband never remarried. Ford's career as a spy was somewhat short-lived, but she was indispensable in one of the more embarrassing events for the Union—the capture of Edwin Stoughton.

CHARLOTTE AND VIRGINIA MOON

Most of the women spies of the Confederacy were devoted to their cause. But many of them, like Charlotte and Virginia Moon, also had vibrant, assertive personalities and could not seem to sit still while a war was raging.

These two sisters became active spies for the South, but they were also actresses with a flair for the dramatic. They were bold flirts who seemed to enjoy committing acts of outrageous daring. Strong

In this April 1865 photo, horse-drawn wagons cross a pontoon bridge near Richmond, Virginia. Pontoon bridges floated on top of the water and could be built quickly, making them useful in military campaigns.

Southern sympathizers, the Moon sisters worked as couriers, crossing state lines and fooling officials with phony accents and disguises. Whether getting expelled from boarding school, crying false tears to unsuspecting Union officers, or working as actresses and writers, the Moon sisters spent much of their lives doing everything they could to defy convention.

Although they were born fifteen years apart, both sisters had illustrious beginnings that pointed the way to their flamboyant careers. At the start of the Civil War, Virginia, or Ginnie, Moon was engaged to sixteen young men. "If they'd died in battle, they'd have died happy, wouldn't they?" she once said unapologetically. "And if they lived, I don't give a damn!"[1]

According to legend, her older sister Charlotte, or Lottie, once left a man at the altar. When asked by the minister if she would take this man for a husband, she paused for a moment, then answered, "No sirree Bob!"[2] and marched out of the church. Perhaps it was a good thing she did. The man she left, a young Ambrose Burnside, would later become a Union general. Burnside would come to be considered a notorious bungler for his delayed reactions that often left his troops vulnerable to risky situations. Having a Confederate spy for a wife would probably not have helped. At any rate, this was not the last either of the Moon sisters would see of Ambrose Burnside.

The sisters were born in Virginia, and although they were raised in Ohio, they remained Southerners in their hearts for years to come. Their father, Robert Moon, was from an old Virginia family. He was a gentle, scholarly man who worked as a physician. Their mother was a rigid Orthodox Presbyterian. Although their parents were respectable citizens, the children were raised unconventionally. The girls read biographies, science, and even Charles Darwin, works that were then considered highly controversial.

As a teenager, Lottie practiced shooting with a gun, rode a horse bareback (without a saddle) through town, and nursed fantasies of becoming an actress. After leaving Burnside at the altar, she married Jim Clark, a suitor much closer to her own age, an attorney who later became a judge. There are rumors that even at this wedding a second suitor showed up at the church thinking it might be *his* lucky day.

When the war started, the entire family rooted fervently for the South. Lottie and Ginnie's two brothers joined the Confederate army. When Robert Moon died, the widowed Mrs. Moon sent Ginnie to Oxford Female College in Ohio, and she herself moved back to Memphis. Lottie and her husband remained in Ohio and became active members of the Knights of the Golden Circle, a secret society with Confederate sympathies. Undercover couriers frequently stopped at the Clark household.

In 1862, a man named Walker Taylor knocked on the Clarks' door. He was traveling from Kentucky under a false name, supposedly to sell mules. In reality, he was an undercover courier, with vital messages to deliver to General Edmund Kirby-Smith in Kentucky. But he was too well known to make the trip into occupied territory, where Union soldiers would be keeping a careful eye on civilian travelers.

Lottie immediately volunteered to make the delivery. She dressed up as a toothless old woman, giving herself a hunchback and wearing a bonnet and a ragged shawl. Convincingly disguised, she crossed the Ohio River by ferry. On the other side, she found a Union transport preparing to leave for Lexington, Kentucky—her destination. A less daring person might have tried to avoid contact with Union soldiers. But Lottie jumped at the chance for a more direct route and perhaps the chance to prove her mettle.

Adopting an Irish accent, she told the soldiers she was trying to visit her sick husband in Lexington and begged them to give her a ride. At first they said no.

Housed at the Library of Congress in the Civil War photographs division, this is a photograph of General Edmund Kirby-Smith, an officer of the Confederate army. Kirby-Smith started out as a lieutenant in the army and worked his way up to general. Though wounded in battles, he managed to see the end of the Civil War and tried his hand at the telegraph business.

But Lottie continued begging, crying, and carrying on, even appealing to soldiers who she thought might be Irish. Finally, the soldiers agreed and smuggled her aboard.

Once in Lexington, she happened to run into a Southerner she'd once met, a colonel for the Confederate army. Straightening up, she thrust the papers into his hand and made him swear he would deliver them to General Kirby-Smith.

With her mission accomplished, she headed back to Ohio on the train, again disguised as the old woman. It was a lucky thing she kept her disguise; once aboard, she overheard that there was a watch out for a female spy. Instead of trying to avoid attention, she promptly began wailing, until a Union general seated near her named Combs turned his head and tried to quiet her. This time her story grew to include hungry children, an ailing husband, and a fear that she would be mistaken for a spy. General Coombs comforted her and promised he would watch out for her safety. When the train arrived in Covington, Kentucky, the general himself gallantly helped this "poor old lady" down from the train. From there she took the ferry home.

After such a stunning debut, Lottie naturally continued transporting messages. Her next big assignment took her to Toronto, Canada, where she picked up documents that needed to be delivered to Virginia. To get there, Lottie pretended she was a British woman and in poor health. She claimed that she was on her way to Virginia's hot springs. With forged papers, she talked her way into obtaining a traveler's pass to Virginia, with an inspired story about how she had crossed the ocean to seek out these curative springs and couldn't die without first trying them.

This photograph, taken by George N. Barnard, shows guards at the ferry landing on Mason's Pass in Washington, D.C., and was taken around 1882. The guards are inspecting travelers' documents.

Pass in hand, Lottie made it to Virginia, delivered the papers, and collected new documents to bring back to Toronto. But she ran into trouble on her way home. Having not actually made it to the thermal springs, she was not well informed on their location. When questioned further, she goofed. Now exposed as a potential fraud, Lottie found herself at the mercy of Union officers. The general interrogating her became suspicious and demanded a surgeon's opinion. Lottie cried and faked her way through the exam, convincing the surgeon that she had severe rheumatism. At the end of the exam, she was taken to her carriage and given another pass.

Lottie's courier activities provided a great outlet for her dramatic personality. She continued acting as a courier until she stumbled upon a former suitor. Dressed again as a British woman in search of the healing springs, she found herself in none other than the office of her old beau Ambrose Burnside. Burnside was now the head of the Union department of Ohio. He was fiercely prosecuting everyone he suspected of Southern sympathies, even old friends. Anyone convicted of aiding the Confederacy could be given the death penalty.

Whether she recognized Burnside immediately is unclear. It is also not clear whether Lottie needed

General Ambrose Everett Burnside, in this painting by Alonzo Chappel, indicates an area on a map. A Union general in the Civil War, Burnside led a trail of several successes. In the war, he captured Roanoke, Virginia, and went on to become the governor of Rhode Island from 1866 to 1869. His final contributions were made as a United States senator from 1875 until his death in 1881.

a pass or was there to convince Burnside to release Ginnie and her mother, who were already in Burnside's custody for their own spying activities.

Regardless of Lottie's intent, she was going out on a limb to be in the presence of a Union general who was making a career of catching Southern sympathizers. She could not possibly have wanted Burnside to recognize her. In this aim, she failed. Burnside listened to her heart-wrenching story about her health and journey and her desperate pleas, whether for a pass or for the release of her mother and sister. Finally, he interrupted. "You've forgotten me," he said. "But I still remember with pleasure the hours I used to spend with you in Oxford."[3] Nervy as ever, Lottie denied ever having met the general. What was he talking about? She was just an British woman trying to get to the springs.

Burnside was not having it, and Lottie finally gave up. Lottie joined Ginnie and Mrs. Moon in captivity. Here she waited to hear if Burnside would exact revenge for his broken heart of thirteen years earlier. Apparently he did not, as there are no records of her conviction. As the war came to an end, so did Lottie's espionage activities. The Knights of the Golden Circle died out. Lottie and her husband moved to New York and lived happily among their former enemies, the Yankees. The war long over, Lottie put her talents to further use as a novelist and a journalist, even traveling to European capitals to cover the Franco-Prussian War.

At the beginning of the Civil War, Ginnie Moon had been kicked out of college. Surrounded by feverish Northern patriotism, she had announced to the principal her wish to leave. When he refused to allow this, Ginnie responded by going outside, taking her pistol, and shooting out every single star in the flag. In this way she won her freedom and prepared to join her mother in Tennessee. While she was waiting, Ginnie stayed with Lottie and Jim Clark. Here, Ginnie received a crash course in the art of spying for the Confederacy. Since she had succeeded in outdoing her sister in gathering fiancés, she was apparently going to try for the same victory when it came to spying.

Eventually, teenage Ginnie made it back to Memphis, where she and her mother tended soldiers in hospitals. Ginnie found this extremely boring. That summer, she watched as Memphis was invaded by Federal troops. There were stories that she took information and supplies to the Confederate troops,

CONFEDERATE NURSES

At the start of the Civil War, it was considered somewhat unseemly for a woman nurse to attend to a wounded man. Nursing had only recently been recognized as a profession in the 1860s, and earlier positions in nursing were frequently held by female volunteers or religious missionaries. At the time, women were at first prone to joining their local Ladies Aid Society, where they spent time knitting soldiers socks, rolling their bandages, or sewing their uniforms.

Innovative women like Ella Newson and Susan Blackford, and programs such as the Women's Relief Society, led the field of nursing on the Confederate side. Recognizing the desperate need for qualified nurses, the Confederate Congress passed legislation in 1862 that allowed for the formal enlistment of female hospital workers. Thus, the Civil War provided the first careers for many women and helped to change their earlier roles in society as homemakers.

After the war, many women who had been involved in the Civil War devoted their energies to the suffrage movement, urging citizens that all adults should have the right to vote.

was arrested, and then charmed her way out—but these stories were never confirmed.

In February 1863, Ginnie learned that the Knights of the Golden Circle needed a courier to take information from Mississippi up to Ohio. Naturally, Ginnie volunteered and convinced her mother to join her, insisting that they would not be suspected, as they had the perfect reason for a trip to Ohio: a family visit. Sure enough, they made it safely to Ohio and delivered the message.

Coming back was more difficult. At that time, Lottie's old beau Ambrose Burnside was heading the Union department in Ohio, making it his business to sniff out Confederate spies. Lottie and her husband were already under investigation. Around the time that Ginnie and her mother were preparing to return to Memphis, an undercover investigator was sent to the Clark residence. He was a charming young man who convinced the Clarks to let him in. In the Clark home, everyone welcomed him, but the agent found nothing—although he did note that the Clarks seemed to work at making quilts morning, noon, and night.

Ginnie and her mother asked their new friend to help them get travelers' passes so they could head back to Memphis. The agent agreed, but he also sent a secret order to the boat captain not to depart until specific orders were received. Ginnie boarded the ship to cross the river looking like any other traveler. Kept secret from anyone else, however, she had a message wrapped in silk and tucked into her shirt. Her bags were also mysteriously heavy, and her skirt drooped.

The hour for departure came and went—and yet the boat remained docked. Ginnie and her mother sat patiently in their stateroom, quite sure they were on their way to complete their mission. But when Ginnie peeked outside of the stateroom, she later wrote, "I saw a Yankee officer coming through the cabin, looking at the numbers on the doors."[4] Upon finding Ginnie's cabin, he asked to come into her stateroom. When she agreed, he surprised her by locking the door behind him. He said he was Captain Harrison Rose and that he was with the Cincinnati Custom House. He had orders to search Ginnie and to deliver her to the provost marshal. He had a note with him that ordered her arrest, calling her a dangerous rebel employed by the Confederate government who had contraband goods and mail for the rebels.

Instead of surrendering, Ginnie reacted with scorn and disbelief. The officer moved to search her, but she stood her ground and all but shouted her indignation. It was almost unthinkable that a male officer would search a female suspect, but Captain Rose was unmoved. Cooly, Ginnie pulled a Colt revolver from the folds of her skirt and pointed it at the captain. "If you make a move to touch me, I'll kill you, so help me God," she told him.[5]

This, at last, was too much for the captain. When Ginnie invoked the name of her old friend Ambrose Burnside, Captain Rose agreed to have her searched elsewhere. He left the room momentarily. Swiftly, Ginnie locked the door, pulled her rolled secret message from her bosom, dunked it in water, and swallowed it. When Rose returned, Ginnie had her hat on and was ready to go.

Pushing through the crowds on their way to find Captain Burnside, Rose remarked dryly to Ginnie, "I suppose you feel like hurrahing for Jeff Davis." Jefferson Davis was the president of the Confederate States of America. Thrilled with her success at destroying the message, Ginnie later wrote, "I raised my hand over my head and said in a loud voice, 'Hurrah for Jeff Davis!'"[6]

Above is a pharmaceutical kit housed at the National Museum of Health and Medicine. It was made by an unknown manufacturer and used in the mid-nineteenth century. The vials contain quinine, calomal, and tannic acid. The most common diseases in the Civil War were dysentery, typhoid, pneumonia, and malaria. Eventual improvements in sanitation and diet in the camps decreased disease but not until after 400,000 soldiers died of various illnesses.

She may have cheered too soon. When their bags were searched, incriminating evidence was found. There were bolts of blue gingham fabric, but this was nothing; Ginnie insisted it was to make children's aprons. (Actually it was to make shirts for Confederate soldiers.) Worse, there were about fifty letters to people in the South—and opium. When questioned, Ginnie shrugged and passed it off to her mother. "Oh my mother can eat that much in a month," she said. Mrs. Moon sat straight-faced, and the officers tried not to smile. In fact, Ginnie confided in them, "She might be under the influence right now."[7]

She might have gotten away with convincing the soldiers that her mother was an opium addict, if not for the additional supplies of opium, quinine, and morphine found sewn inside Ginnie's unusually heavy collection of quilts. These were substances the South desperately needed to treat wounded soldiers—and highly incriminating evidence to be found on someone suspected of sympathizing with the South.

As if it weren't abundantly clear at this point that Ginnie Moon was working for the Confederate cause, another discovery sealed her fate. Her hoop skirt got caught in the door, and when a soldier helped her to brush it out of the way, he noticed that it was strangely heavy. A housekeeper was called into the office to search Ginnie. Sewn into her skirts were forty bottles of morphine and seven pounds of opium and camphor.

After this shocking discovery, Ginnie could not complete her journey. She and her mother were placed under arrest. Ginnie pressed for decent

BITING THE BULLET

Unfortunately for wounded soldiers, the English surgeon Joseph Lister would begin his research on the use of antiseptics in surgery just one year after the Civil War ended. Civil war surgeons' preferred method of treatment on the battlefield was amputation. They used the same knife on every soldier, wiping the blood off onto dirty aprons between surgeries. Although some anesthetics were in use at that time, most doctors did not know how to administer them, nor did they have the supplies on hand.

Consequently, Civil War surgery usually meant being laid onto a bloodied board with a tub underneath, sometimes being offered a shot of whiskey and a bullet to bite. Then the wounded limb was removed. Under such conditions, a good surgeon was a fast surgeon. After enduring this ghastly operation, many soldiers died anyway, from infection or gangrene.

Others, packed into filthy overcrowded camps, died from diseases spread through sewage-infested drinking water. All told, about twice as many Civil War soldiers died of disease than of battle wounds.

accommodations. (Prisons were not considered suitable for women.) When she learned that General Burnside was staying at the Burnet House, she insisted that she and her mother be brought there.

At the hotel, Ginnie settled into a decidedly cheerful version of prison life. Almost immediately, Captain Rose asked her to dinner. Ginnie responded cheekily, "Well, you're my jailer. I have to put up with you!"[8] While they dined, Rose held up a telegram and teasingly asked if she would like to know what was inside. They were in a hotel dining room. Ginnie knew he wouldn't make a fuss in public, so she snatched the telegram out of his hand and opened it. Inside was a message from a general in Nashville, ordering that Ginnie be sent to him.

But in the morning, Ginnie demanded a meeting with Burnside. Although it had been thirteen years since her sister had left him at the altar, Burnside was kind to Ginnie. He assured her he would try her himself. This left Ginnie greatly uplifted, and she began enjoying her period of confinement. She sometimes teased the Yankee officers, accusing them of stealing her undergarments. "I had not the slightest idea that my stockings, petticoats or *corsets* could be construed as *government prizes,"* she exclaimed.[9]

Soon Ginnie was being invited down to the hotel lobby to visit with staff officers. The pretty eighteen-year-old was being entertained so well by the Union men that she raised eyebrows. She later wrote, "The Yankee women in the parlor looked very indignant to see their officers being so polite to a [Southern] woman."[10]

She was even asked to a play by a young Northern officer. When she responded that leaving the hotel would mean breaking parole, he sought permission from General Burnside. Ginnie waited eagerly for word that permission had been granted, then promptly refused to go. "My brothers are in front of your bullets daily," she said. "I wouldn't be seen escorted by a Yankee!"[11]

Charges against Ginnie were eventually dropped, and she returned to her life as a Confederate supporter. Evidence of her espionage eventually reached as far as Philadelphia, Montreal, and Nashville, though she was never convicted of any crime.

In the middle of 1864, she tried to leave the United States to join her brother in France, where he was waiting out the war. Along with her brother's wife and two children, she made the trip as far as Newport News, Virginia, before being stopped by Union officers. They demanded the women take a Union oath. Ginnie's sister-in-law complied, but Ginnie snorted at the request and refused. She was held in custody for a period before being asked to take the oath again. Still, she refused. Exasperated, the officers released her into Confederate territory.

In Memphis, Ginnie lived out most of her days, an eccentric Confederate supporter even decades after the South lost the war. For years she dressed in old-fashioned silks and hats and never married. In her seventies, she decided to become an actress and headed west, where she acted in bit parts alongside the likes of Douglas Fairbanks, a world-famous actor of the silent-film era. Still later, she moved to Greenwich Village in New York City, where she chain-smoked, drank mint juleps, and told of her past exploits. She died a vibrant spinster in 1926, at the age of eighty-one.

MARY SURRATT

Mary Eugenia Surratt did not seem a woman intent on contributing to a cold-blooded assassination. This mother of three was a landowner, a widow, and the owner of a boardinghouse in Washington, D.C. She was also the first woman to be executed by the United States government.

But was Surratt a treasonable spy, guilty of conspiring to murder President Abraham Lincoln? Or was she merely the victim of circumstantial evidence and the

unlikely recipient of a shocked nation's outrage? Historians have debated the matter for well over a century and will probably continue to do so for many years. Ultimately, Surratt was accused of conspiring with Confederates and running a safe house for Confederate sympathizers.

Born Mary Elizabeth Jenkins in Maryland in 1823, Surratt grew up on a farm. Her father died when she was just two years old. When she was twelve, Surratt was sent to a Catholic boarding school in Alexandria, Virginia. Five years later, at seventeen years of age, she married John Harrison Surratt, the son of a wealthy planter. The couple inherited land outside of Washington, but a fire destroyed their property in 1851. Still, they continued to be prosperous. Two years later, they purchased 287 acres (116.1 hectares) of land, where they built a tavern, a post office, and a polling place. It was also where they raised their three children, Isaac, Anna, and John Jr. By 1854, Surratt's tavern had grown to include lodging for local travelers and was later called Surratt Hotel. The tiny community that formed around their holdings was eventually known as Surrattsville.

In August 1862, Mary's husband died. And although he seemed like a successful business-man, he left her in debt. Unable to maintain the

Mary Surratt's home, seen here in a photograph taken between 1890 and 1910, was converted into a boardinghouse around 1864. One of her most famous boarders was the Confederate assassin John Wilkes Booth.

property herself, she decided to rent the tavern in Surrattsville to a former policeman named John Lloyd. Little did she know this man would turn on her in her greatest hour of need. Meanwhile, by 1864, she moved into another house that she owned, this one in Washington, which she had converted into a boardinghouse.

Even though Maryland and Washington, where the Surratts lived, were both part of the Union during the Civil War, many of their neighbors supported the South. Two of Mary's sons actively showed their support. Her eldest son, Isaac, joined the Confederate army, and her other son, John Jr., became a Confederate courier.

As a courier, John mingled with many fervent secessionists. One of them happened to be John Wilkes Booth, a young man from a well-known family who would become famous as Abraham Lincoln's assassin. But by the time Booth made his first visit to Surratt's boardinghouse, on New Year's Day in 1865, his plan was not to murder the president. Instead, he wanted to kidnap him. Booth had already discussed his plan with Mary's son John, John's friend Louis Weichmann (a boarder at Surratt's house), and a physician named Samuel Mudd. Because he knew the area, John Surratt Jr. agreed to guide Booth and his proposed

hostage across the Potomac River. But two kidnapping attempts failed. By March 25, after many visits from Booth, John Jr. told his sister, Anna, that the actor was crazy. He

This photograph of John Wilkes Booth (1838–1865) was taken in 1863. Before Booth shot President Lincoln, he was a famous actor who was highly acclaimed for the many Shakespearean roles he played.

This portrait of Mary Eugenia Surratt (1820–1865) was made in 1865, the same year Surratt was hanged with other conspirators who, it was thought, met to plan President Lincoln's assassination. Some people believed there was insufficient evidence to convict Surratt and were horrified that a woman was sentenced to hang.

asked her to tell Booth that he was not home.

On April 14, 1865, the day of the assassination, Mary Surratt was traveling to Surrattsville with Louis Weichmann. As they were preparing to leave, Booth showed up at the boardinghouse and handed Mary a package to give to one of her boarders, John Lloyd. (It was said in the trial that the package contained field glasses.) When she found Lloyd, he was drunk. This did not stop him from later testifying that Mary had instructed him to have whiskey and "shooting irons" ready for whoever might show up that evening. Indeed, that night, after shooting the president, Booth showed up at Lloyd's tavern.

Weichmann and Lloyd were both arrested, and after being kept in solitary confinement and threatened with being charged for Lincoln's death, they both agreed to testify against Mary Surratt. On the night of April 17, 1865, Surratt herself was arrested and taken from her Washington boardinghouse to the Old Capitol Prison. Within weeks she was transferred to the Washington Arsenal Penitentiary, where Lincoln's assassination trial was later held.

The proceedings began less than one month later, on May 9.

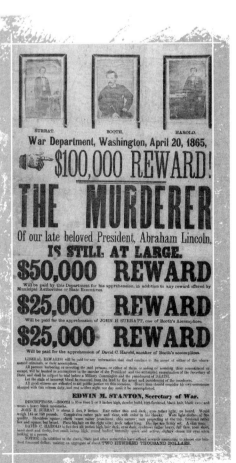

This broadside offers a $100,000 reward for the apprehension of President Lincoln's murderers, who, as of April 20, 1865, were still "at large." At the top of the poster are photographs of John H. Surratt (left), John Wilkes Booth (center), and David Herold (right).

These Colt revolvers are two of the four firearms found in the possession of President Lincoln's assassin, John Wilkes Booth, after he was shot and killed on April 26, 1865. Booth's other firearms were the Derringer pistol he used to shoot the president and a Spencer carbine rifle.

Weichmann testified that he had seen the accused men—John Wilkes Booth, Lewis Powell, George Atzerodt, and David Herold—meeting in Mary Surratt's boardinghouse. But Weichmann also testified that he had never heard Mary express anti-Union sentiments. Friends and neighbors showed up in court to support this claim. Surratt was found guilty of conspiracy after her tenant, John Lloyd, became a key witness. As expected, he testified that Surratt had requested he secure both field glasses and carbines (small firearms) for Booth and Herold on the night of the assassination.

On June 29, 1865, Mary Surratt, Lewis Powell, George Atzerodt, David Herold, Samuel Mudd, Michael O'Laughlin, Edman Spangler, and

This photograph depicts the four Lincoln conspirators moments before they were put to death by hanging on July 7, 1865. Surratt *(behind the parasol)* was hanged along with Lewis Powell, David Herold, and George Atzerodt. Her last words were, "Don't let me fall."

Samuel Arnold were found guilty of conspiring to assassinate the president. Surratt, Powell, Atzerodt, and Herold were sentenced to be hanged.

Although numerous appeals were made on Surratt's behalf, they were either ignored or never received by President Andrew Johnson. Awaiting a pardon, Surratt was hanged in Washington, D.C., on July 7, 1865, along with the three others. She went to her death proclaiming her innocence.

TIMELINE

February 4 – Six seceding states form a provisional government, the Confederate States of America.

February 9 – The Confederate Provisional Congress elects Jefferson Davis as its president.

March 4 – Abraham Lincoln becomes the sixteenth president of the United States.

April 12 – Confederate troops attack Fort Sumter, in Charleston, South Carolina. The fort is surrendered the next day.

April 15 – President Lincoln issues a call for 75,000 men to do a three-month stint in the army. (Blacks are rejected.)

April 19 – President Lincoln calls for blockade of Southern ports.

May 21 – Richmond, Virginia, is declared the Confederate capital.

July 21 – The South wins the First Battle of Bull Run.

August 5 – The federal income tax is introduced.

1862

February 6 – Fort Henry in Tennessee falls to the Union.

February 25 – Nashville, Tennessee, comes under Union occupation, debilitating the South.

April 6–7 – Both North and South suffer tremendous losses at the Battle of Shiloh.

April 16 – Jefferson Davis signs the Conscription Act, the first military draft in the history of the United States.

April 18–25 – Union troops occupy New Orleans.

May 4 – Union general McClellan and his troops occupy Yorktown, Virginia, and go on to Richmond.

TIMELINE Cont.

August 27–30 – Under Lee and Jackson, Confederate troops win the Second Battle of Bull Run.

September 17 – Confederate troops are massacred in the Battle of Antietam, the bloodiest day in U.S. history. Lee aborts his plan to invade the North.

September 22 – Lincoln issues a preliminary Emancipation Proclamation, to take effect on January 1, 1863.

December 13 – Burnside and his Union troops are defeated at the Battle of Fredricksburg.

1863

January 1 – The Emancipation Proclamation is issued by Lincoln.

January 25 – The 54th Massachusetts Volunteers become the first Northern black regiment.

March 3 – The Union passes a draft law, though hired substitutes, or $300 payments, are allowed in lieu of serving.

June 22 – The newly formed state of West Virginia is admitted into the Union.

July 1–3 – The turning point in the war: Southern troops are defeated in the three-day Battle of Gettysburg.

July 4 – Vickburg, Mississippi, falls to Northern troops, giving complete control of the Mississippi River to the Union.

July 8 – Port Hudson, Louisiana, is occupied by the North.

July 13 – There are draft riots in response to the Union draft laws. The most violent occur in New York.

November 19	Lincoln delivers the Gettysburg Address.
1864	
March 9	Ulysses S. Grant is named general in chief of the North.
May 3	Grant advances into Virginia with 120,000 troops.
May 4	Union general William T. Sherman advances toward Atlanta, with 110,000 men.
June 1–3	Grant and Lee come head to head at the Battle of Cold Harbor in Virginia. Both suffer tremendous losses.
June 7	Lincoln is nominated for a second term, in spite of his lack of popularity.
June 30	Congress passes the Internal Revenue Act to raise money for the war.
July 5	Horace Greeley, a New York editor, receives a letter that suggests that Confederate delegates in Canada are ready to discuss peace. Lincoln sends an emissary, but the talks fall apart.
September– December	Sherman marches through Georgia to the Atlantic Ocean, from Atlanta to Savannah.
September 2	Sherman takes Atlanta. The city is burned and ravaged. Civilians are ordered to leave.
October 13	Maryland abolishes slavery by a narrow margin.
November 8	Lincoln is reelected.
December 22	Sherman arrives in Savannah.

TIMELINE Cont.

1865

January 11 – Missouri abolishes slavery.

January 31 – The House passes the Thirteenth Amendment, abolishing slavery. It goes to the states for ratification.

February 22 – Wilmington, North Carolina, the last of the Confederate ports, falls to Union forces.

March 2 – Lee calls for negotiations, without surrendering first. Lincoln refuses the request until surrender comes.

March 13 – Out of desperation, Jefferson Davis signs a bill to allow blacks to enlist. Few actually join.

April 3 – The Confederate capital, Richmond, falls to the Union. Lincoln tours the city and is cheered by former slaves.

April 9 – Lee officially surrenders to Grant at Appomattox Courthouse, Virginia.

April 14 – Lincoln is shot in Ford's Theatre. He dies the next morning.

April 15 – Andrew Johnson is sworn in as president of the United States.

April 26 – John Wilkes Booth, Lincoln's assassin, is shot and killed in Port Royal, Virginia, while trying to escape his pursuers.

July 7 – Mary Surrat is hanged in Washington, D.C., along with Lewis Powell, George Atzerodt, and David Herold.

Glossary

abolition A movement to abolish, or end, slavery. A person opposed to slavery was known as an abolitionist.

acquit To discharge completely from accusation.

allegiance Devotion or loyalty to a person, group (such as a government), or cause.

amnesty The act of an authority by which a pardon is granted to an individual or group.

bombard To attack with artillery or bombers.

bravado The act of showing off; a false sense of bravery.

camphor A natural crystal compound taken from the wood or bark of the camphor tree that was sometimes used as a topical painkiller during the time of the Civil War.

cipher A method of transforming text in order to conceal its meaning.

civility A polite act or expression.

Civil War The conflict from 1861 to 1865 between the Northern states (the Union) and the Southern states (the Confederacy), which seceded from the Union. Also known as the War of the Rebellion and the War Between the States.

Confederacy The eleven Southern states that seceded from the United States in 1860 and 1861; the South. Members of the Confederacy were called Confederates.

coup A brilliant or sudden upset.

Emancipation Proclamation A declaration issued by President Abraham Lincoln that called for the end of slavery in the United States. Issued on January 1, 1863, during the third year of the Civil War, it declared that "all persons held as slaves are and henceforward shall be free."

espionage The act of spying.

genteel Elegant or graceful in manner or appearance; upper class.

Gettysburg Address A speech given by Abraham Lincoln during the Civil War on November 19, 1863, at the dedication of a national cemetery on the site of the Battle of Gettysburg.

incense To arouse the extreme anger or indignation of another.

indignant Having anger that is caused by unjust or unworthy actions.

lassitude A condition of weariness or fatigue.

Louisiana Purchase A 885,000 square mile (2,301,000 square kilometer) region of the western central United States that was purchased in 1803 from France.

martyr A person who sacrifices his or her own life for the sake of a principle.

morphine An addictive narcotic drug that is sometimes administered to relieve extreme pain. Morphine was available during the Civil War, though not widely.

myriad A great number.

opium A bitter brownish addictive narcotic drug that consists of the dried juice of the opium poppy. Opium was also available during the Civil War, though not widely.

quinine A natural crystal compound taken from the bark of the cinchona tree that was used to make a medicinal tonic during the time of the Civil War.

ratification The act of approving a law or amendment.

secede To withdraw from an organization.

treason An act of betrayal, especially to one's government.

Union Northern states loyal to the federal government headed by President Abraham Lincoln during the Civil War; the North. Members of the Union were called Federals.

veteran A former soldier.

For More Information

The Civil War Preservation Trust
1331 H Street NW, Suite 1001
Washington, DC 20005
(202) 367-1861
e-mail: info@civilwar.org
Web site: http://www.civilwar.org

The Museum of the Confederacy
1201 East Clay Street
Richmond, VA 23219
(804) 649-1861
e-mail: info@moc.org
Web site: http://www.moc.org

The National Civil War Museum
One Lincoln Circle at Reservoir Park
P.O. Box 1861
Harrisburg, PA 17105-1861
(717) 260-1861
Web site: http://nationalcivilwarmuseum.org

U.S. Army Women's Museum
2100 Adams Avenue
Building P-5219
Fort Lee, VA 23801-2100
(804) 734-4326
e-mail: AWMWeb@lee.army.mil
Web site: http://www.awm.lee.army.mil

Washington Civil War Association
P.O. Box 3043
Arlington, WA 98223
(800) 260-5997
e-mail: rebgunner@elvis.com
Web site: http://www.wcwa.net

WEB SITES
Due to the changing nature of Internet links, the
Rosen Publishing Group, Inc., has developed an
online list of Web sites related to the subject of
this book. This site is updated regularly. Please
use this link to access the list:

http://www.rosenlinks.com/aww/conf

For Further Reading

Cutter, Barbara. *Domestic Devils, Battlefield Angels: The Radicalization of American Womanhood, 1830–1865.* DeKalb, IL: Northern Illinois University Press, 2003.

Eggleston, Larry G. *Women in the Civil War: Extraordinary Stories of Soldiers, Spies, Nurses, Doctors, Crusaders, and Others.* Jefferson, NC: McFarland & Company, 2003.

Garrison, Webb. *Amazing Women of the Civil War.* Nashville: Rutledge Hill Press, 1999.

Hillstrom, Kevin, Laurie Collier Hillstrom, and Lawrence W. Baker, ed. *American Civil War Primary Sources.* 2 volumes. Detroit: UXL Gale Group, 1999.

Mikaelian, Allen. *Medal of Honor: Profiles of America's Military Heroes from the Civil War to the Present.* New York: Hyperion, 2002.

Savage, Douglas J. *Women in the Civil War.* Philadelphia: Chelsea House, 2000.

Bibliography

Bakeless, Katharine, and John Bakeless. *Confederate Spy Stories*. Philadelphia: J. B. Lippincott Co., 1973.

Boyd, Belle. *Belle Boyd in Camp and Prison*. Baton Rouge: Louisiana State University Press, 1998.

Campbell, Helen Jones. *Confederate Courier*. New York: St. Martin's Press, 1964.

Chang, Ina. *A Separate Battle: Women and the Civil War*. New York: Puffin Books, 1996.

Davis, Kenneth C. *Don't Know Much About the Civil War*. New York: William Morrow, 1996.

Garrison, Webb. *Amazing Women of the Civil War*. Nashville: Rutledge Hill Press, 1999.

Greenhow, Rose O'Neal. *My Imprisonment and the First Year of Abolition Rule at Washington*. London: Richard Bentley, 1863.

Halacy, Dan. *The Master Spy*. New York: McGraw-Hill, 1968.

Jones, Katharine M. *Heroines of Dixie: Confederate Women Tell Their Story of the War*. New York: Greenwood Publishing Group, 1955.

Kane, Harnett T. *Spies for the Blue and the Gray*. Garden City, NY: Hanover House, 1954.

Kinchen, Oscar A. *Women Who Spied for the Blue and the Gray.* Philadelphia: Dorrance & Company, 1972.

Leonard, Elizabeth D. *All the Daring of the Soldier: Women of the Civil War Armies.* New York: Penguin Books, 1999.

Mahoney, M. H. *Women in Espionage: A Biographical Dictionary.* Santa Barbara, CA: ABC-CLIO, 1993.

Pember, Phoebe Yates. *A Southern Woman's Story.* Jackson, TN: McCowat-Mercer Press, 1959.

Scarborough, Ruth. *Belle Boyd, Siren of the South.* Macon, GA: Mercer University Press, 1983.

Simpkins, Francis Butler, and James Welch Patoon. *The Women of the Confederacy.* Richmond, NY: Garrett and Massie, 1936.

Stern, Philip Van Doren. *Secret Missions of the Civil War: First-Hand Accounts by Men and Women Who Risked Their Lives in Underground Activities for the North and South.* New York: Bonanza Books, 1990.

Underwood, Rev. J. L. *Women of the Confederacy.* New York: Neale Publishing Company, 1906.

Wert, Jeffery D. *Mosby's Rangers.* New York: Simon & Schuster, 1990.

Source Notes

Introduction
1. Francis Butler Simpkins and James Welch Patoon, *The Women of the Confederacy* (Richmond, NY: Garrett and Massie, 1936), p. 5.
2. Elizabeth D. Leonard, *All the Daring of the Soldier* (New York: Penguin Books, 1999), p. 93.

Chapter One
1. Harnett T. Kane, *Spies for the Blue and the Gray* (Garden City, NY: Hanover House, 1954), p. 18.
2. Kenneth C. Davis, *Don't Know Much About the Civil War* (New York: William Morrow, 1996), p. 17.
3. Ibid., p. 191.
4. Rose O'Neal Greenhow, *My Imprisonment and the First Year of Abolition Rule at Washington* (London: Richard Bentley, 1863), pp. 23–24.
5. Ibid., p. 29.
6. Ibid.
7. Ibid., p. 56.
8. Ibid., p. 25.
9. Ibid., p. 290.

Chapter Two
1. Belle Boyd, *Belle Boyd in Camp and Prison* (Baton Rouge, LA: Louisiana State University Press, 1998), p. 49.
2. Ibid., p. 50.
3. Ibid., p. 82.

4. Ibid., p. 105.
5. Ibid., p. 106.
6. Ibid., p. 107.
7. Ibid., p. 110.
8. Ibid., p. 133.
9. Ibid., p. 145.
10. Ibid., p. 146.
11. Ibid., p. 149.

Chapter Three

1. Elizabeth D. Leonard, *All the Daring of the Soldier* (New York: Penguin Books, 1999), p. 95.
2. Ibid., p. 45.
3. Harnett T. Kane, *Spies for the Blue and the Gray* (Garden City, NY: Hanover House, 1954), p. 171.
4. Ibid., p. 173.
5. Leonard, p. 49.
6. Ibid., p. 49.

Chapter Four

1. Harnett T. Kane, *Spies for the Blue and the Gray* (Garden City, NY: Hanover House, 1954), p. 263.
2. Ibid., p. 263.
3. Ibid., p. 274.
4. Ibid.
5. Ibid., p. 275.
6. Ibid., p. 266.
7. Ibid., p. 277.
8. Ibid., p. 266.
9. Ibid., p. 277.
10. Ibid., p. 278.
11. Ibid.

Index

About the Author

Larissa Phillips is a freelance author living in New York City.

Photo Credits

Cover (left), pp. 28, 31, 43 © Bettmann/Corbis; cover (middle top,) pp. 21, 24, 41, 44, 57, 58, 69, 71, 88, 93 Prints and Photographs Division, Library of Congress; cover (right), pp. 49, 54, 63 Manuscript Division, Library of Congress; cover (middle bottom), p. 90 Rare Book and Special Collections Division, Library of Congress; pp. 6, 55, 56 © Corbis; pp. 10, 16, 37, 73, 91 © Hulton/Archive/Getty Images; pp. 26, 46 Rare Book, Manuscript, and Special Collections Library, Duke University; p. 35 (top) © Corbis; p. 35 (bottom) © Mark E. Gibson/Corbis; p. 51 © University of North Carolina at Chapel Hill; p. 60 Library of Congress; p. 66 Civil War Photograph Collection, Library of Congress; p. 80 National Museum of Health and Medicine; p. 89 © Picture History; p. 92 © Tria Giovan/Corbis.

Designer: Evelyn Horovicz; **Editor:** Joann Jovinelly; **Photo Researcher:** Adriana Skura